# The God Thing

## Susan Millar DuMars

salmonpoetry

Published in 2013 by
Salmon Poetry
Cliffs of Moher, County Clare, Ireland
Website: www.salmonpoetry.com
Email: info@salmonpoetry.com

ISBN 978-1-908836-25-0

COVER PHOTOGRAPHY: *'Still'* © *Susan Prediger*
COVER DESIGN & TYPESETTING: *Siobhán Hutson*

*Printed in Ireland by Sprint Print*

*Salmon Poetry gratefully acknowledges the support of The Arts Council*

*For Mary Higgins,*
*1942-2011*

*and for her son,*
*my husband*

# Acknowledgements

*The Moth*; *Skylight 47*; *The SHOp*; *Crannóg*; *Burning Bush II*; *The Recorder* (US); *Raintown Review* (US); *Mosaic* (anthology, Skylight Poets, Galway); *Dogs Singing: A Tribute Anthology* (Salmon); *The Poet's Quest for God* (anthology, Eyewear Publishing, UK).

'Proof 'was commissioned by the *Pamphlet Project*, which brings together writers and visual artists in collaborative ventures. For more information, visit: www.facebook.com/thepamphletproject

'The Leaving' was written during sessions of the *Poetry Depot*, in which members of the public ask poets to make poetry of their experiences. For more information, visit:
www.spiritstorelimerick.weebly.com/poetry-depot.html

I'm very grateful for the help of Susan Prediger; Hannah Kiely; the Skylight Poets, past and present; Ed Boyne; John Walsh; Dave Rock; Susan Lindsay; Marcella Morgan; Rebecca O'Connor; Ronan Scannell and everyone at Away With Words; Dr. Robyn Rowland; my dad, visual artist Donald DuMars; and my stepmom, Catherine Bonner. Special thanks to Milo Prediger, whose hands grace the cover.

A very personal thank you to all those who came together at #13 in May, 2011.

And my constant love to Jessie Lendennie and Siobhán Hutson of Salmon Poetry; and to my husband, Kevin.

# Contents

## IV: *Earth*

## V: *Prayers*

*All poetry is prayer.*
SAMUEL BECKETT

*air*

# Harm

A yellow-grey ghost in too-big pyjamas,
she feels her way along the hall.
I offer my arm, but that isn't
what she wants to hold onto.
*Kevin. And Helen.* Names she whispered
in their ears when they were born.
Years of accumulated magic
in the sounds. *Helen. And Kevin.*
*Why don't they phone each other*
*more?*

I could tell her
a reason; the ways
she got it wrong,
caused harm.
Hell, I've carried
that speech unsaid
for years. Could wield it now.
"The reason those two
don't trust, is you. Is you."

But she has reasons too.
I know the harm caused her,
know the shape it's put on her,
can see it now,
even now,
when the hallway
stretches long.

There's hurt enough.
No more harm.
I drop the speech, hold out my arm.
All the words we haven't said,
are curtains to be slid aside;
she lets me help her into bed.

Then I sit sideways in the leather chair
beyond her door, listening
for cough, cry,
wince – I'm convinced
I'd hear a wince –
I'm nothing but a giant ear.
No further harm will come to her
while I am here

while I am here.

# If I Was Good

If I was good, I'd tell you to love
this hush;
if I was a better person, I'd know how to say
that God is in this silence. But what use to you,
this silence?
Hasn't God got anything
to say?

If I was good, I'd help you to reach
your God.
I'd have faith to weave into
a ladder.
If only I was good, but I'm
no good –
God really should have sent you
someone better.

# Clasp

He fixes my necklace clasp.
His fingers trace me,
skimming thin skin of neck,
full flesh of shoulder.
A breeze of a touch
to let me know
though we now
measure hours
in her liquid
morphine doses,

he is still mine.
I am still the future,
his, to clasp.

# Near the End

Her face all bone and eyes.
She always looks surprised.
Sucks the air's marrow,

pushes beans around her plate.
I push words around
this page.  Both have gone cold.

All this white space
is where we pause,
fight for breath.

# I'm Always Running Into Him These Days

His hands are cold, he needs
a shave.  In the breeze,
his red scarf flaps. *You love me*,
he says smugly, *think about me
constantly.  Admit it:
I shape your days.*

He tugs my wrist.
Each step I take toward
him makes colours ripen,
sounds deepen;
the crust of frost
on the grass
crunches
white.

*Where will I turn up next,
you wonder.*

I gaze into the face of Death.
His red scarf flaps in the breeze.

# Undiscovered

We lie together quietly
in our big boat of a bed.
His toenail, kneecap, hipbone,
the warm, wet tang of him.
The familiar soft spell
of his voice. *Now that I've seen death,*
*I don't know how anyone*
*can think there's a God.*

I see what he is seeing:
the final clench of jaw, the last
mute struggle, the leak of colour
starting at the hairline.
The way the lips fall open,
dumb. The nurse tucks a rolled cloth
beneath the chin to close the mouth.
*We're machines, we break down.*
*Nothing more. Nothing else.*

I remember her body
just after – shrunk,
the skin a new skin,
cold and slack as a white sail
on a windless day.
Something had gone. Though we can't
see the breeze, we know when
it stops blowing. Something had gone.
I only want to know what it was.

# Nothing In This Life

Away from her sickroom
the colours blind me.
I walk into people,
get entangled,
snagged on sharp points of conversation.
Then music – one note

trembles mid-air.
Faces rush past. The note breaks open,
a song like rain
spills into empty spaces.
I could drown
in remembering.
A radio song for car journeys,
inner journeys, walkman soundtrack.
I'm convinced the sax player knows
what he's doing, in secret
language talking to me

about final journeys.
People fling coins at his
old black case.
I stop,
remember Mary

waking, sobbing.
*Open it*, gasping, *open it*.
I tore at the curtains,
shoved out the window,
filled her room with breezes,

traffic sounds, light.
I held her hand.
Small wet breaths
we breathed together. At stake
not just her life
but life.

I'm crying
in the middle of Shop Street
because all of this
will go. This gorgeous confusion.
The song will end.
The street will empty.
Nothing in this life is as hard
as leaving it.

*water*

# Pattern

*There are ninety-nine words meaning God in the Qu'ran.*

Across a wet, white moon
clouds, like petals, scattered.
Ninety-nine names for God
written in their pattern.

# For the Woman Who Goes to the Well

I know you feel small,
a nut or a seed
that gets caught
in the teeth;

know you feel burned
by this all-seeing sun
and by unkind eyes
and flame tongues.

I know shame sticks
like dust to sweat –
know you crave
a cool bath.

But you wait
till the sun's at its height
and no one's about
to go to the well.

I know you dream
of water.
The bucket's splash
like laughter.

Your palms marked
by rope
when you hoist
the bucket up.

To you it's like
collecting stars
from the depths of the sky.
It's just that far

to reach what you need,
to fill the bath
with something clear and clean
like truth.

But you wait
till the sun's at its height
and no one's about
to go to the well.

# The First Blue Nude

In Matisse's bathroom
they've found the first
of the *Blue Nudes*.

A framed photo of Lydia[*]
taken through a blue filter.

She sits on a lawn
in a long summer dress,
looking at him.  Her bent knee
a mountain,
her raised arm a circle.
She smoothes her hair.
The filter turns her ink-blue,
the grass beneath her a rippled lake
and each blade-drop
almost touchable.
She is smiling
with her eyes, her lips
the most patient, perfect smile.

He kept her in the loo
so he could see her from his bath.
His hairy, veined,
waning body
cradled by her gaze.

She indulged
the man who could not stand
inside the frame but only

to one side, looking.
Who saw her as shapes arranged,
an intact egg.
Saw her
always new, as though
he'd just sketched her in.

And she's saying, *Alright, Patron.*
*Take the picture.*

* Lydia Delectorskaya, model and
  companion of Matisse in his later years.

# White Sock

We talk over your tumour
at your kitchen table.
The side effects of chemo.
Yes, I'll have more tea.
No, don't get it,
don't trouble,
I can fill the kettle.

When I get up I see your trouser hem
trapped inside your white sock.
Suddenly I'm sweating.

The sock is sinister,
swallowing your cuff.

The sock is laughing
at my chit-chat
hand patting
two cups of tea and I'm away
tick ticking you
off my list of things to do.

The sock is mocking
your foil wrapped biscuits,
fridge magnet maxims.
The sock knows better.
The sock tells the truth.

I turn away,
wait for the water to boil.

# Stevie Nicks In The Women's Locker Room

She's piped in, belting it out.
We change with our backs to the room.
*Stop dragging my –*
red marks left from waistbands,
shy glances through the steam.
Fragile ribs, the secret skin.
Shoulder blades stretch and cave.

Stevie gives it all she's got.
*Stop dragging my –*
Inner thighs, fingers, toes.
Each unhooks her bra.
Tom Petty too,
but he's just support –

and then all together –
*stop dragging my –*
into our hairbrushes –
*stop dragging my heart around!*

The mirror fogs.
Towels to the tiles.
We laugh loudly.

# Learning to Swim

*for Mary*

### i.

Reach and then kick and then kick and then
breathe in the clean smell of chlorine.
The ripples of light making circles
to thread with my body.

So what if you won't take your pill?
If you clutch at your stomach but won't let me help?
And I kick and then sputter and spit;
no good at this.

### ii.

Next day I find you entangled in stockings and bra.
How to look without looking, be matter of fact?
I have to be brisk
or we both will be broken.

*Come here, Cinderella*, I say when I finally
put on your shoes. It's time to make tea so I hold
both your hands and walk backward; like teaching
a toddler to stand. Thus we shuffle along.
*What must we look like?* I say. We're laughing.
You reply: *We look like we're dancing.*

*iii.*

A week later, you're gone.

I do twenty laps.
Pulled through the water like thread
in a stitch. As I get out, I feel
nothing but small,
on the edge
of that open space.

What have I learned?
Don't forget to keep breathing.
Don't try to move water. Let the water
move you.

# Grief

I'm reading the future.
Time's ticker-tape unspools.  Ice veins
in the river of my hair.
Like you, I've moved past pain.
It's cold here.
Time unspools, entangles.
I'm reading the future
       and it's more
         of the same.

# Wreckage

I've lost myself at sea;
trudge the winter shore,
mutter scattered bits of prayer,
wait for word on me.

Salt clouds.
Sand abandoned.
The sea a distant black tantrum.
My fingers shriek with cold.

If they find me –
amongst my wreckage, clinging blindly –

will it still be me?
Or the waves, will they
have changed me?

# To the Bone

*Budgetary constraints are believed to be preventing DNA testing of bones found off the south-east coast which may have come from some of the fishermen lost when three trawlers sank in 2006 and 2007.*

IRISH EXAMINER, 4 September, 2012

On sunny days he'd roll the window down,
rest his elbow on the frame, at ease
behind the wheel – I'd watch
the sun paint patterns on his freckled
bulk of forearm –
all the way home.

So how can you not tell me
if what you've found –
rubbed white by tides,
dried by that same sun –
whether that length of polished bone
was once my husband's arm?

# Wallace Hartley's Last Moments
# Aboard The Titanic

*for Michael Diskin*

And what has made your life
worth living?
As the deck pitches
and water reaches
past your knees
and the sky is sharp
with stars, but not one
that can lead you home.
What has made this life
yours?

Don't look for God, but
yourself;
if He is anywhere,
He's in your answer.
The tune you play
as the ship goes down.

Longer than the screams, the prayers,
the crack and gush and groan,
longer than the pop of signal flares,

we will hear your song.

*fire*

# What I Most Recall About the Funeral

That gold coffin hinge
the sun stirred to life
as you and the other men
bore your mother up the aisle –
your sister and I behind,
arms full of flowers.

Above the darkness
of your straining shoulders
that shiver of metal,
so bright.

# Matisse Near the End

An artist is an artist
in his striped pyjamas
in his bed on the brink of hell
or heaven – the two, after all,
are close together.

When Icarus falls
in flurries of sparks
he has in his ribcage
the flame that started it all.

An artist is an artist when he stops caring
what anyone else thinks.

When, near the end,
he draws Icarus,
Matisse has the eyes of God,
fire inside his own ribs,

the outstretched arms
of a falling man.

# The God Thing

Oh God, in whom I can't believe:
murderer.
Forsaker.

God in whom I won't believe:
pissed off
sack of thunder.

God in whom I once believed:
loving Father.
Maker.

God, I wish I could believe.

Help me.
Feed this hunger.

# They Put Down Ronan's Neighbour's Dog

*for Ronan Scannell*

He'd bitten someone's leg.
Not 'put down', *killed*,
that's how Ronan says it,
*killed him.  Great fucking dog.*
Ronan, can you sit down?
Ronan, please don't curse!

Ronan says he wants to be
a big dog.  White.
And what would this dog say?
*He'd bark, he'd HOWL.*
*Chase cats, BOW-WOW-WOW.*
*He'd dig up your garden.*
Ronan, can you sit down?

*Bow-fucking-wow.*

# Hotel Insomnia

Now we wander
corridors of thought,
each room a numbered
womb in which gestates

a grievance whimpering
in sleep – waking soon.
Tiny fingers, nails.
Scratching half-moons.

# Poor Daddy

*Alas! my daughter — for I have opened my mouth unto the Lord, and I cannot go back.*

General Jephtah, *Judges* 11:35

Was it in the middle of the night? Were you frightened?
The only one in camp awake? Did the sky look on in silence
as you prayed for a sign? God should know better,
Daddy; the night before a battle
is a nervous time. You're likely not to sleep,
to make promises others must keep.
Poor Daddy.

Let the blade fall — let the flames consume
my new breasts, my virgin womb.
Daddy, tell me I'm pretty in my long white robe.
I'll be pretty forever now, Daddy! Don't sob.

Forever I'll belong to Him
and you, my Daddy.

# Madame Matisse Is Shown Her Portrait, 1913

Whose is this face?
A pebble thrown in a pond,
sinking grey over black over grey,
further and further away.

Whose are these hands?
Fingers unfinished; flippers to flap
around garden and house.
My hands are stronger than that.
Counted coins, wrote ferocious letters,
once. Don't you remember?

Why that hat?
With blushing rose
and peacock feather.
What does that sexless creature
need with a Paris hat?
Why not a dowager's veil,
a housemaid's cap?
Why not a wimple and beads,
my Lord!
The better to toil toward
your veneration.

I'm a good disciple, you will allow –
everybody loves you now.

Why these tears? Why this feeling I'm sinking?
*Portrait of Madame Matisse.* Who is she?
Henri, my love, my dear old friend.
When did you stop seeing me?

# Photo of my late mother-in-law, New York, 1963

I'm sorry I laughed when you showed me this;
didn't realise your pride in that girl,
cool and pink as peppermints.
To me you looked like a white Supreme,
homesick Beauty Queen,
not as lovely as you
became.

We're two blue-eyed daughters of Irish Marys
who called themselves *May*
and breezed off the ferry
and got their hearts squashed by Yellow Cabs.

Girls like us, with mothers like them,
forget who we are –
find clues in photos,
others' reactions.
So I'm sorry I laughed.
I see it now –
you were fresh
as peppermints.

# Two Women

### i.

Yesterday's Woman blinks
in bare naked sunlight.
She wears a housecoat,
wrings her hands.
*Child, why are you*
*out here alone?*
*You'll be raped by coyotes,*
*cancered by sun.*
*You'll get lost in this desert*
*and miss all your favourite TV!*
Her voice is smoke rings
and the smoke rings are lassoes
and the lassoes hog-tie me.


### ii.

Tomorrow would be
more at home in winter.
She wears a chunky scarf
around a bent stem of neck.
She writes in invisible ink,
throws the pages up to heaven;
snowstorm in reverse.
Stork-steps across the sand to me,
tied up tight, light of pocket.
Shrugs the shrug of infinite sadness.

Tomorrow has nothing to say.

# Hopper's *Sun in an Empty Room*, 1963

Autumn's long hands
rattle glass panes,

its palms press the darkness
into corners –

darkness, darkness is brother
to light.  Each makes the other

easier to love.
The old artist gives

us walls buttered with sunlight,
blocks of heat,

pooling on the floor –
and shadows.  Nothing more.

Gold and umber shade
lie quiet side by side.

Nothing, nothing is brother to all.
Winter is sister to Fall.

The old artist knows
as the world falls from sight,
we're left with just our darkness –

and the light, the light, the light.

*earth*

# New Year

Red saplings suckle
at the milk sky.

The spine-sharp old shrub
births a single sunset rose.

Hope hurts me, prickles
like blood returning.

# Healing

*Daughter, thy faith hath made thee whole.*

MARK 5:35

the white cloth blooms red
smears her thighs
stains her fingers
as she lifts it sticky
with her own juice heavy
with her own juice soaked
with her own juice sighs
replaces it with dry white
rinses the inner skin
pain drags her
belly low feasts
on her belly
as it has every day
for twelve years

she stumble shuffles
feels the drip
down low unclean
stumble shuffles
people move
aside sideways eyes
say unclean
hiss unclean
she sees him
speaking to many
it must be him
           she

                    reaches
                              for
                                    him

And when her hands tangle
in the softness of his cloak
and when his eyes linger
softly on her face
she remembers –
remembers who she is.

*It's me*, she says.
He smiles.
*It's you.*

# View from Hannah's Window

Hopper would paint that little white
seaside house, right now —
the sun low,  the house
like the moon,
every colour, no colour, white
that's a sound; laughter,
feminine.  Satisfied.  Red
door and driveway gate.

He'd use this, make your eyes slide
side-to-side, red to red.  Invent
a woman standing by the gate.
Apron over white dress.
Red hair lifted by the wind.
Head down; face hidden.

And though the sea is naked lips
of white and rushing blue behind,
you will not remember this.
When you close your eyes you'll see
the house that stands alone and bright;
the thin, hard arms of the red-haired woman
closing her gate for the night.

# Folds

Autumn erases the sky
so I take down the old brown
coat, revisit its folds,
the drag and swish through town
last Christmas. The cold
last Christmas.

A bent train ticket,
a cough sweet wrapper
in the left hand pocket.
Time folds. Remember –

winter had packed up the sky,
and I, last Christmas,
was so bloody cold.

# From the Window of the Train

### *i*

Five men wait in their coats
in an empty yellow lot.
The morning's cold.
Manassas, Virginia.

### *ii*

Two curled in sleep
on woodchips by the tracks.
One wakes, his face an old face.
His eyes, when he looks at us, young.

### *iii*

Sudden steep red earth.
Headphones soundtrack your journey.
Mine as quiet
as these trees.

### *iv*

The ridge hugged by track.
The train recollects the mountain.
The mountain
remembers.

# On Arrival

*Dublin Airport*


The choir of faces
I've longed to see.
My step-dad leans
on a bin. Mom has her hair

like it is in that photo,
*Cornwall, 1984.*
Rob stands apart. Kim in
her *Carpe Diem* tee shirt.

Alex talks to Chuck
and Chuck looks great
for someone who died
in 2004. Still has the beard.

And I look again and they are different,
strangers. Their eyes sweep past me
searching for the one they will claim,
their lips puckering: "Welcome".

And I look again and am different,
different even from the woman
who boarded the plane. Somehow smaller.
Older. It's not that I dislike

travelling alone. It's just when I see
rows of expectant faces behind
the barrier, it makes me
want to have something to claim,

for all the miles,
besides baggage.

# The Leaving

*for Sarah*

Massive blue and white striped
shirt, worn by your mum
when pregnant with you.
By your dad, who's always
tallest in the room.
Even now, when he's ill –
even viewed from this distance.

Worn by you
when you felt a bit
shit, needed something
to hide in.  Saw
you through the Leaving Cert,
leaving home.
Now, you're leaving all
of us – Ireland.

You're shaping your life.
Life is shaping you.
The shirt?
Without noticing,
you've grown into it.

*Written with Sarah Maria Griffin as part of the InkStorm Poetry Depot at National University of Ireland, Galway in May, 2011.*

# To The Fair

Turn on the moon,
the white winking moon.

Turn on the lamps,
those black stemmed lamps
with their heavy bright fruit
so they drip lemon light again.

The wind will lift my hair.
The Clare hills
a painted backdrop,
blue and distant as death.

We'll lick ice cream
and head to the fair.

Let me see us again
as I saw us then.
Let us find answers
in Garibaldi biscuits.

It goes so fast.

The seagulls laughing.

The Ferris wheel turns.

# The Lydias
*for Kevin*

When your shadow sibling breathes fire,
threatens our home, I want to fill the place
with red apples till they overflow
their basket, roll across the floor,
chased by our cat.  Fill it with cats,
self-possessed, soulful, stretching,
yawning on sunlit blankets.  Fill it
with blankets, woolly, striped, warm.
I'm feathering a nest for you
because I believe in you –
in me
believing in you.

When Hitler breathed fire,
threatened their home, Lydia filled it
with oranges and lemons, seashells,
songbirds for Matisse to paint.
Filled it with heat for that achy old man
and his naked young models.
She kept him serene
in their flat overlooking
the red roofs of Nice.
Saw her value
by seeing his.
And Matisse made pictures.

When the old guard breathed fire,
threatened disciples, Lydia of Acts gave
shelter; filled her home
with prayers, purple fringed cloth,
meat and wine and salt and shade
and bluebells. Believed
in herself believing in baptism.
And the disciples preached.

This is what we do. The Lydias.
We don't waste time shaking fists at heaven,
but choose who to love, and build them a haven.
That is our value.

# Secret Wings

*for Cathy*

My step-mom phoned to tell me
I'm an angel.
Her psychic told her.
Said I'm very tall. *I'm five foot six,*
I say. *Average.*
She is not deterred. The psychic said
I'm an old soul.
I picture angels young.
Cherubim, I realise.
Gabriel – barefoot, hand on heart,
kneeling before Mary to tell her his message.
Even the flowers
lift their heads to listen.
That's an angel.

*The psychic said it wasn't your time*
*to come back.*
*You chose to –*
*there was something*
*you wanted to do.*
Now I'm wondering what it was.
Have I done it?
Am I doing it now? It's Sunday,
I bought groceries and now I'm listening
to my step-mom who's in Arizona, where
new shades of green grow, just beyond her porch,
in the clean white heat
of her nurturance.
That's an angel.

I've never been an angel. Not even
in a Nativity play.
One Halloween I dressed as a priest.
I went to a party and everyone there
wanted to confide in me.
I liked it, like listening.
Though the collar was too tight.

If I'm an angel
maybe all of us are angels.
No white tunics
or expressions beatific.
Telephones for trumpets.
Secret wings.

# Geelong

four a.m., the room hot
twisted sheets
his snores mock

step outside, barefoot
stones still
hold warmth

look up

moon soft
as a split avocado

spilt sugar stars

can't believe
this was waiting for you
all you had to do
was step outside

# Proof

They're on a bus. She looks
out the window. Sees
herself, miles moving through her.
Neck girdled by concrete divider.
Mouth of rushing meadow.
Trio of power lines
threaded through her eyes.
Thinks:
*the view is you.*

And how can we prove/disprove
anything, when
we look out, see in?
See, in everything,
our own reflection?

She wants to ask him:
*How do I know*
*blue is blue*
*to you?*
*Is your blue*
*my blue too?*

She doesn't ask

because they're on the bus
to their common
destination.
Whatever
about heaven,
she needs to believe
they share blue.

# Between Us Apes

The kiss, I guess,
goes back to Mama Monkey,
tongue-tidying. Think of this;
I could be sucking nits
from your pelt when I pucker, press.

Nits are not nice
and I only want niceness
to linger on my mister.
Yes,
I mean you, Monkey Man.
Kiss kiss.

# Pumpkin Song

Carve me eyes to see the sun
slant, breaking gold
on bark and stone.

Blaze my thoughts with wonder,
my love with ember words;
apple, smoke, river.

I would be a lantern,
flicker bright through throbbing woods –
path nettle-tangled.

I would be a lamp
holding back the skirts of night
till we clear a place to camp.

Carve for me a mouth
and I will sing away the darkness;
put a tune to truth.

# Mint Plant

It unfolds its rough patterns,
reaches towards a distant light.
The sun in its sky not as perfect
as the prayers of each leaf.

*prayers*

# Sunday Morning, Lorient

There's a man wiping down the carousel
as if it's the only thing that matters.
Beneath his white rag flattered panels
blush and flash like fallen sections of sky.

There's an old man up on his balcony
wrapped like something precious in his white robe.
He's looking at the church across the square.
The air so still he can hear the choir.

A pine cone rattles to the cobbles.
Jackdaws, and the warm wood of this bench
expanding as though with breath.
Small white roses grow on the square,

their fluttering faces like candles.
I need no other cathedral.

# Prayer of a Good Listener

I've tried to soak up
all the hurt,
grown fat on anguish.
It was what I thought
You wanted. You, who made me
able to bear
many times my weight
in sorrow.

I want You to tell me
I've done right.
With You,
I can be small again.
Pink petals ecstatic
in summer rain.

# Who Art in Heaven

*for Thom*

A father dies; his son is seven,
mind pink and curled as a seashell,
full of echoes that could be music.
The boy with his small hands
traces the empty space that used to hold
his Dad. And he asks the grownups, *why?*

"He watches over you every day. He will
never leave you." And comforted grownups
go back to grownup things.

The boy draws lines connecting his memories
and the memories are stars and the lines mark
a constellation he's told is Father. But between
the stars and lines there is

nothing but sky.

# Hopperville

*for Edward Hopper, American artist, 1882-1967*

Sad, restless creature, this city –
never knows when to stop talking.
Turns the night brittle with cheap
bangles of light, the stink of gasoline,
pink cologne.  Cha–cha music
braided with crap radio hiss.

Between hot pavement and hard, starless sky,
windows – rows of bright rectangles.
Framed in these,
the city's hostages.
Sleek winged things sleeved in blunted flesh.
Each has sore feet, bowed head,
hands that reach for newspapers, keyboards,
other hands.

We see them when we look up,
glimpse them in ritual,
blessing themselves by brushing their teeth,
boiling the kettle.  Haloed
by laptop light, oracled
by weathermen, prayed for
by talk show hosts, tested
by alarm clocks and empty beds.
Broken.  Holy.
Each of God's reflections
turning out the light.

# Aspects of God

*after Weldon Kees*

God orders another and asks that Sky News
be turned down; too easy to confuse
with prayers, that monotone of misery.
The sounds of now and history
merge for Him, sometimes, into one plea.
Even the olive in His martini
beseeches Him; He slides the toothpick
from its flesh, bathes its wounds, licks
vodka from His fingers. The olive sinks.
*I can't keep going like this*, God thinks.

God in the lobby tries to look sober,
head bowed, chin in His collar.
Yesterday's men wander, rummaging
in pockets, muttering like moth wings;
beat, beat, they circle the light.
Taxis draw up outside,
and with every turn of the doors
there's more.
Grey, gone men.
Ghosts, vapours.
God shows them to glass elevators,
pushes buttons for them,
shrugs off their thanks.
Lift load by lift load He brings them upstairs,
tells them *stand back from the doors,*
*and don't be scared.*

# Leaving Coldbath Street

You mock belief in God;
yet it's you who believes in miracles.

You think you can leave Coldbath Street
all at once —
that a star-white spirit,
pound notes in her hair,
will lift you above council flats,
the shuffly silent queues
of light rail travellers.

Let me tell you
no one leaves Coldbath Street that way.
It takes one shy step every day,
one step
toward whatever trembles
with truth
for you.

If not God, then the way turned soil
smells of rain, but sweeter.
The way the azalea's roots
cleave to the ground.

If not God then the Higgs-Boson particle
or half-remembered lines from *Desiderata*
or the woman beside you on the bus
who crosses herself at the sight of a hearse.

If not God, the silence
of a Connemara road.
The romance
of dark chocolate on the tongue.

If not God, then first words.
Last words.
The ordinary transactions of flesh
with which we honour what's beyond all flesh.
My husband never more of a man
than when dabbing with a wet sponge
his dying mother's lips.

You mock me for searching
for God in people.
Even if I don't find Him
what better way to love them?
You only sit in a pew
so people will approve.

Let me tell you:
no one leaves Coldbath Street that way.

# The Wishing Bell

*Church of the Assumption, Bled Island, Slovenia*

Here is how you make a wish:
cross the green lake of dreams,
climb the ninety-nine steps
of aspiration.
The sun, your father, praises you.
The church, your mother,
offers you shade.

Dare to put what you most want
into words.
Pull the rope.
Ring the bell.

The tolls that once told us
when to pray, sleep, gather, grieve
resound now to say you've arrived
at this moment of openness.
This moment
of asking.

# This is How You Say Goodbye

Not the day the yellow rose sighs
as it lands on the coffin lid.
Mourners murmur in awkward clumps
among gravestones. And someone says,
"Nice day for it."

Not then but some ordinary dusk,
nothing on telly. You leave off the lights,
lie on your back, watch out the window
the gulls fly in dizzy circles,
white belly grey wing.
*Rain is coming*, you say to yourself.
And it comes. And it's like the world
let out its breath. You open the window
on cooled air and battering, battering,
your own breath faster now;

and in your mind's eye, a rowboat
on the shore,
the wood warm,
the name once
lovingly painted on its side
rubbed away.
But you know the name.

The rain and your breath raging, but
on that shore, it's peaceful. Calm water,
open sky. With one lunge you push
the rowboat into the waiting water.
Simple. Sand grates against the bottom

and then the water receives it, sweetly,
irrevocably. Watch it carried out,
bobbing, lifting, until it's very small,
the sea vast, your hands empty.

This is how you say goodbye.
This is how you start
to breathe properly again.
Watch the rowboat
until it disappears.

Photograph © Susan Prediger

SUSAN MILLAR DUMARS' debut poetry collection, *Big Pink Umbrella*, was published by Salmon Poetry in 2008; *Dreams for Breakfast* appeared in 2010. Her work features in *Landing Places*, Dedalus' 2010 anthology of immigrant poetry written in Ireland; and also in *The Best Of Irish Poetry 2010*. A fiction writer as well, she published a collection of short stories, *Lights In The Distance*, with Doire Press in 2010. She has been the recipient of an Arts Council Literature Bursary for her stories. Susan has performed her poetry in Ireland, Northern Ireland and the UK; in Athens and in Brittany; in New York, Chicago, St. Louis, Denver, Washington DC and Huntington, West Virginia; and in Geelong and Canberra, Australia. Several of her readings abroad have been sponsored by Culture Ireland. Susan teaches creative writing to adults at various academic venues; and to individuals with special needs through the Away With Words project. She and her husband, the poet Kevin Higgins, have run the acclaimed Over the Edge readings series since 2003. Susan and her husband were the subject of a documentary, *Rhyming Couplet*, made by Des Kilbane in 2009. Born in Philadelphia, Susan now makes her home in Galway, Ireland with Kevin and their cat, Ziggy.